Ending the Cycle

Ending the Cycle

A 14-Lesson Plan to Changing your Life

Douglas McKoy, Jr.

Library of Congress Control Number:		2021911154
ISBN:	Hardcover	978-1-6641-7763-5
	Softcover	978-1-6641-7762-8
	eBook	978-1-6641-7761-1

Print information available on the last page

Rev. date: 05/26/2021

To order additional copies of this book, contact:
Xlibris
844-714-8691
www.Xlibris.com
Orders@Xlibris.com
829779

CONTENTS

Foreword...ix

Preface xi

Lesson 1   Inside the Frame: Understanding who you are 1

Lesson 2   Feelings and Attitudes 6

Lesson 3   Changing Your Thoughts.................................9

Lesson 4   Re-examining Motive: Shifting from Unrealistic
            to Realistic Thinking 12

Lesson 5   Violence Prevention 15

Lesson 6   Repair and Reunite.......................................19

Lesson 7   Changing Behaviors (Life Skills)...................23

Lesson 8   Enough is enough 27

Lesson 9   Successful People vs. Unsuccessful People 29

Lesson 10   Pre-Release Preparation Part I.......................32

Lesson 11   Stage One: Job Readiness..............................36

Lesson 12   Learn to Live Stress Free 40

Lesson 13   Pre-Release Preparation Part II:
             Creating the Master Plan 43

Lesson 14   What's Your Purpose? 46

Final Thoughts 49

Bibliography 51

After reading the book I learned that the book could not just be beneficial to prisoners and people getting out of prison, but the book can work for anybody. The book teaches how to solve problems to deal with everyday issues that we all go through in life. I recommend this book for anybody including myself and my children. Everybody needs to be critical thinkers this is another book that would definitely assist you in that process along with my three favorites: *Think and Grow Rich*, *As a Man Thinketh* and *Richest Man from Babylon*. This book sums all 3 of those up. You definitely should take the time out and check it out. Problem solving is a very, very important technique in life. Once you know how to solve problems, there is nothing you can't do. So take the time out and check out this book. I guarantee, you will find it just as rewarding as I did. Peace.

- Freeway Rick Ross

FOREWORD

The *Ending the Cycle: A 14-Lesson Plan to Changing your Life*, book by Douglas McKoy is a thoughtfully crafted, easy to read, step-by-step guide created for pre-released inmates within correctional institutions. Mr. McKoy, RAS, RES. understands the importance of pre-release programming and the need to remove barriers that effects inmates upon post-released, reintegration into their respected communities. He also understands the attitudes of society and the resiliency needed by formerly incarcerated people to make it successfully in their communities. The 14 lesson plans are essential for psychological rebuilding.

Incarceration is a form of deterrence for those who committed crimes. Punishment is a form of negative reinforcement for the crime(s) committed. And, rehabilitation is defined as the act of restoring, in this case the offender, to an original state, however, there are many variables involved attempting to do such, yet no one ever returns to an original state, but can changed their lives through mentoring, coaching, education, social modeling and self-help. *Ending the Cycle* is a self-help workbook that invokes the psyche to remember, relieve, walk through, understand, accept, forgive, prepare, set goals and plan, and take small steps in achieving change.

Ending the Cycle's overall premise provides an inmate a road map to discovering his or her purpose in life. This is the most overlooked, invisible goal of all therapeutic modalities, purpose. Many inmates do not have a purpose, not alone understand why one exists, and *Ending the Cycle* creatively builds to that point and this is very creative of the author Mr. Douglas McKoy. A book that needs to be within every correctional institution in the US and abroad, *Ending the Cycle,* would aid in the educating of inmates and decreasing recidivism while growing safer communities!

Sincerely,

Frank T. Williams

Frank T. Williams, MA. MS. is the director of the Senior Ex-Offender Program in San Francisco, the first of its kind program in the nation, focusing on older adults. Mr. Williams is a formerly incarcerated person who turned his life around 18 years ago. He holds Master Degrees in Humanity and Leadership, and in Criminal Justice and is currently a Ph.D. Candidate at Northcentral University. He is a certified substance abuse counselor (1999) under California Association of Alcohol and Drugs Educators CATC-IV. He has received numerous awards from local, state and federal officials for his work within the community and the criminal justice systems.

PREFACE

Hello Ladies and Gentlemen,

My name is Douglas McKoy. I wrote this pamphlet with the intent of providing you all wisdom on your journey. Being incarcerated does not mean that you wait until you are free to make a change. On the contrary, being away from the insanity that is your life is the perfect time to examine yourself. I speak from experience; for you see 25 years ago, I was, like you locked up.

I was confined to an institutional life determined not to have an institutional mind. Upon my sentencing, I made up my mind to do my time and to never return. It has been a challenging journey, but I am happy to report that I have never returned. I am also happy to return that there are several men and women, who like me, have made the same successful transition. We are a testimony to the fact that you do not have to remain a criminal because you have made a mistake. You can change your life. The power is in you.

This 14-lesson booklet is a culmination of a journey fulfilled. I have wanted to share with you secrets of success from a soldier who has made the journey.

Your current situation, being incarcerated, has not brought you much success. Why not try something new? You won't know if it can work, until you work it.

Stay Up,

Douglas McK

Changing Criminal Behaviors: One Mind at a Time.

Introduction:

This 14-week lesson plan is designed to help those currently incarcerated in county jail to consider the consequences of his or her actions. Participants are asked to examine his or her self in an effort to improve their attitude, thinking, and behavior.

Lesson 1:

Participants examine themselves: understanding and accepting who he or she is and how they see his or herself "inside the frame." This is a concept that asks the participant to remove the self-constructed perspective, to consider what influences or factors cause him or her to see them in the frame.

Lesson 2:

Participants will examine his or her feelings and attitudes towards themselves and the world around them. The impact of how one feels cannot be underestimated; our feelings drive our attitude and influence our actions. This section will explore the consequences of both feelings and actions.

Lesson 3:

Participants are asked to see themselves in relationship to society. It's the power of the individual thought and how those thoughts influence him or her. The questions ask participants to explore why they are here.

Lesson 4:

Inmates begin a transformative look at their thoughts. "Shifting from unrealistic to realistic thinking" is about making a change in the way they view themselves. The goal is to shift from negative thinking to positive thinking.

Lesson 5:

The group is asked to consider why they are angry and how that anger affects those around them. Steps are provided for consideration in avoiding violence.

Lesson 6:

Participants are challenged to repair and reunite with loved ones with whom he or she may have a damaged relationship. This lesson further asks them to understand his or her role in the relationship building process.

Lesson 7:

Time is spent on improving life skills of participants. In order to achieve some degree of success upon release, the participant has to change his or her mind about how he or she is living. This chapter gives them areas to consider when creating change in his or her life.

Lesson 8:

This week the class affirms that it is time to put the past behind him or her in order to move on. Change is imminent.

Lesson 9:

Considering the difference between successful people and unsuccessful people is the difference here. Inmates examine the attitudes between successful person and an unsuccessful person. He or she is asked to consider plans upon release.

Lesson 10:

Participants are asked to consider plans after being released. They are provided with an overview of an effective plan towards being released from jail. It's part 1; part 2 will be covered in Lesson 12.

Lesson 11:

Participants examine his or her job readiness. This lesson will explore what it means to be job-ready. It's designed to get inmates in the mind of seeing themselves getting ready to work after jail.

Lesson 12:

Participants consider how he or she will face challenges that may seem insurmountable. With that in mind, lesson 11 encourages him or her to learn how to live stress free.

Lesson 13:

Participants will create a realistic plan that he or she can complete upon release. The chart is designed for the individual to take proactive steps in drafting a realistic goal for his or her life.

Lesson 14:

In the final lesson, individuals are asked to consider his or her purpose. This is the final examination of the inmates' goal for his or her life.

In closing the objectives of this booklet are to actively engage inmates in changing his or her mindset and thereby, changing his or her behavior. The first step one must take before actively engaging in any form of change is acknowledging that change is necessary. To that end, it is an inside-out process; participants must be mentally prepared to make the changes necessary to have the life he or she wants to have. The tools in this booklet are small steps in realizing his or her dream.

LESSON 1

Inside the Frame:
Understanding who you are

The first step towards change is to understand and accept who you are. The focus therefore is on change. In order for change to occur, we must first recognize the problem (within ourselves, our environment, & others); we must own it (yes, the problem does exist); and admit that it is causing some problem in our lives. Accepting your reality means acknowledging that you are responsible for your situation. This is the first step in creating change.

Behavior:

Behavior is defined as the actions of an individual. Our behavior is influenced by what we've been taught and what we've experienced. Triggers are reactions based on social or personal factors; they impact your behavior in motion. You act or react to certain things based on what your education, experiences, or instincts have taught you. Anger is an emotion but the reaction to that anger is a behavioral response. In this case, your response to that anger is a negative reaction, which may or may not have a negative influence upon your behavior.

Think about it: a crime of passion is usually a negative reaction to someone or something that has hurt you. When one commits a violent crime, his or her behavior is negative or counter social norms. But what influenced him or her to commit the crime? What caused the negative behavior?

Questions for Consideration:

1. What behaviors have hurt you?

2. Why did you act that way?

3. Were you lashing out? Acting silly (immature)? Or a victim of your own poor decisions?

Inside the Frame:

A frame is a border that encloses an object in, it sets it in place. The borders hold it together, in other words it imprisons the picture and keeps it from moving out of place.

In many ways, you are that picture. Mentally, you have built a vision of who you are; it can be a nostalgic image of your past self, a romantic image of your ideal self or distorted image of yourself now. No matter the image, a frozen image of one's self is hard to change if the mental frame renders you immobile. Understanding who you are is difficult to see from the inside out.

Think about it. A picture freezes a moment in time. So when you are looking at that picture, you are looking at an image of who you are in that moment. The frame holds up the picture. Many of you are trapped inside of a frame that pictures you as a gangster, a robber, a thug, a drug addict, a prisoner or a victim. Yes, a victim, you've given yourself over to your circumstance. You are trapped inside of your frame.

Trapped inside the frame is conditional thinking. It is based on a condition that renders the individual helpless to the external and internal forces in his or her life. The external are the people, environment and events that have influenced or shaped one's beliefs and actions. The internal is the mind: the things you tell yourself you need to do survive.

Everyone is likely to experience conditional thinking; it has influenced, shaped, or motivated everyone's actions at some point in time. The difference between those on the outside and those on the inside are the things that they tell themselves and the things they choose to do to survive.

How does one eliminate the negative forces behind conditional thoughts? That's a tough question, but only the individual true to his or herself can find the answer.

Questions for Discussion:

1. What is your frame?

2. What influences shaped or positioned your frame?

3. What experiences did you create while in the frame?

4. What are the effects of your frame?

5. How does the frame still influence your life?

6. How can you change your frame?

LESSON 2

Feelings and Attitudes

In Lesson 1 you considered behavior and attitude, this lesson explores the impact of feelings on you.

Feelings are emotions and their accompanying sensations. Happy, sad, angry, love, and hurt are all emotions that impact your life. If a situation occurs that you like, you are happy. When a loved one dies, you are sad. When things don't go the way you think they should, you are angry. When you meet someone and they excite you, you are "in love;" finally, you are hurt or disappointed when that same someone leaves. Feeling and emotions influences how one thinks and acts. There is connectivity between your thought process and your feelings and between your feelings and your actions.

Whatever the case is, whenever the emotion arises, the common denominator is you. You control the key to your emotions and responses.

An important step to changing your lifestyle is recognizing who you are. Why you feel the way you do? Why you think the way you think? Self-awareness empowers you to control how you change.

Question: How do your feelings impact your decision making?

For Discussion:

Case Scenario: If you were expecting an important phone call and your inmates are aware of it, how would you feel if he or she did not let you use the phone or did not pass on the message?

Questions for Consideration:

- How would you feel about it?
- What would your attitude be towards your inmates? Why?
- How would that attitude affect your relationship with him/her?
- What actions would you take towards your cellmate?
- Why would you react this way?
- What would be the impact of your actions?

Questions for Discussion:

1. Are the consequences worth the action?

2. Can you change your feelings about the situation? If so, how? If not, why not?

3. Can you change your attitude?

4. What is an alternative solution to my initial reaction?

5. How would this new resolution benefit you?

LESSON 3

Changing Your Thoughts

Psychosocial refers to the relationships or connections between an individual's thinking and the relationship within his or her social environment. In other words, it's the study of how one's thoughts effect his or her social actions and interactions.

Thoughts are powerful.

Never underestimate the power of your thoughts; they create life and can cause death. Thoughts such as fear, anxiety, anger, and doubt can ruin a person's life. Just as thoughts like bravery, peace, happiness, and confidence are thoughts that can improve one's life. The thoughts you have not only influence how you live, but with whom you associate. If you think you are no better than where you are, then that's where you will stay; however, if you think you are better than your circumstance, then chances are, you will climb yourself out of that situation. The mind is a powerful tool, our thoughts emanate from deep-seeded beliefs and values that influence our behavior. Controlling how you think, changing what you think and being open to new thinking will improve your situation.

Every criminal, every person confined to an institution is there because his or her thoughts and actions put him or her there. They are there because they chose to believe or think that this is all they can do or are worth. Naturally, then your current station is where you are supposed to be. But it does not mean that it's where you have to stay or return to, you have to change your thoughts. Ownership of the problem that you've created is the first step in changing your thinking.

If you can't change your situation, then change your mind about it. You don't have to settle for circumstance. Jail is a temporary condition. Your thinking has the power to make it a continual situation or to give it permanent erasure from your life. **You can rise above it.** By establishing and executing a positive attitude, you can change your station. Remove the greatest obstacle first: your thinking.

Questions for Discussion:

1. Why are you here?

2. What thoughts influenced your decisions that brought you here?

3. Where did your criminal behavior come from?

4. Is your chosen lifestyle, criminal behaviors, is it working for you? If yes, then why are you here? (Do good criminals get caught?) If no, are you ready to change?

5. What do you need to do to change?

6. What role does letting go have in creating change?

LESSON 4

Re-examining Motive:
Shifting from Unrealistic to Realistic Thinking

In order to avoid returning to jail, the criminal must shift his or her thinking from a negative or unproductive state to a positive productive state. The negative state of mind usually tends to dwell in unrealistic thinking. Negative thoughts are usually born out of lifestyles, beliefs, or environment. Most people who are locked up did not always think negatively, but poor decision making has had a negative impact on their lives.

Consequently, they are at some point incarcerated, addicted, injured, or dead as a result of negative thinking. Their minds are trapped in an unrealistic world. They tell themselves they will use just one more time, they will only run with this crowd just a little while longer, or that they aren't really hurting anybody, they are doing them a favor. These are negative thoughts based in an unrealistic world the individual has created for his or her self. If you are, as you are reading this, saying to yourself that you had no choice that the drug called out to you, or if you didn't do it your "friends" would have done you, or that is just the way of the game, then you are still stuck in an unrealistic world view. The question is how do you change it?

Now you may ask, why do I need to change? Well, take a look around at your conditions? Think about that question, when you are lying in a bunk next to a cellie/bunkie or several cellies/bunkies. Is this where you really want to be? Do you really want someone telling you when to eat, when to shower, when to go outside? Is this lifestyle okay with you? If yes, then cool, nothing said here will work for you, but, if you say no. No and that you want something more and something different, then making a lifestyle change, shifting from the unrealistic to realistic thinking is good way to begin.

Shifting from negative to positive is not easy. It requires discipline and energy. This is important to understand at the outset as you are changing your lifestyle. You are changing decades of negative thinking and behaving. Think about this way, if you gain 100 pounds over a six year period, it cannot take you six days or even six months to shed it all away. You have to work on it daily to rid yourself of the unwanted weight. Negative thoughts are negative weight sitting on you, effecting how you see, how you think, and how you hear. These areas in turn, affect how you think and how you act. A thought is a thought until you move towards making it a reality.

Setting goals in life is a key to success. If you were to ask any successful person how goals rank in their being successful many would say high. The key to setting goals is to set goals that are realistic or obtainable. Set a goal you know you can achieve. Setting small measurable goals helps the goal setter see progress and motivates him or her to move forward. For example, one measurable goal now would be to complete a chapter of book you've been reading for a while. You tell yourself: *I am going to complete this book in a week; I will read 2 chapters a day. Similarly you can set a goal towards others: I am going to do some kind act every day for one week.* No one has to know your goals but you. If you execute this successfully, without negative thinking, you will see your thinking slowly start to change. Negative people or thinkers let life impact them, while positive thinkers impact life. Everyone has problems, everyone has negative thoughts; the difference is the way one acts or reacts towards it.

The key to change is developing a consistent pattern of practiced behavior and practiced thinking. It is not going to happen overnight, but it will happen.

Questions for Discussion:

1. Identify any negative thoughts that you have.

2. What is the impact of your negative thoughts?

3. List three negative thoughts you want to change?

   a.

   b.

   c.

4. Set three realistic goals that you can reach?

Goal	Time Table	Outcome

Set obtainable goals by clearly stating the goal you want to accomplish, a reasonable timeline in which you can get it done and the outcome. The chart provides a visual aid for you to measure how well you are meeting your goals. You can modify this to your understanding. The key is to keep a goal sheet and complete it accordingly.

LESSON 5

Violence Prevention[1]

There is an irony to this week's lesson. *Some will ask, how do I do that? Why is it important? Or how do I survive without some violence? It's my survival technique.* Violence may be nothing new to be many of you; as a matter of fact, for some it can be a way of life. But, aside from surviving the last bullet, knife, or fist fight, how is violence working for you now?

Violence comes in many forms. Some believe it is just a physical act, but it can also be mental and verbal. Aggressive behavior seldom begins with a positive state of mind; it is often a deep-seeded negative or painful thought or feeling that when provoked causes the individual to respond angrily. This anger manifests itself through physical, mental, or verbal acts of aggression. Understanding the source of your violent reactions is important in understanding how to prevent it.

Moving beyond violence is necessary for the individual to avoid making the same mistakes. Think about your response to the questions above. How many times did you bury your pain or your anger through alcohol or drugs or both? How many times did you take out your uncontrollable violent mental state on your girlfriend, wife, or children? When your anger escalates to physical or verbal acts of aggression it suggests that you lack the desire or strength to control it. Yet controlling it is necessary in order to survive.

The great myth is that many believe reacting violently makes them feel better. They tell them things like: *It feels good to hit a wall or a punching bag. It feels good to curse someone out. It feels good because it's me against the world. Life has not given me anything so should I care?* The angry individual takes their frustrations out on others but more importantly they take it out on themselves. When the addict uses, who are they hurting? When a person kills or beats a person to death or just short of it, who do they hurt? The obvious answer is the victim but the deeper answer is his or her self. For example, when you react violently in jail, you add more time to your sentence. Only the person so deeply hurting doesn't care. No one wants to be locked up. No one wants to be encaged.

More than controlling the temper, violence prevention is about understanding the source of the pain. That's why the questions above are so important. In order for you to change externally, you have to understand what's going on internally. What do you tell yourself to survive? How do you respond when others say things that offend you? How many of the situations that you've been in, short of self-defense, warranted a violent reaction? Once you can be honest with yourself, then you exercise the patience and control you need in avoiding violent confrontations.

Steps to avoiding violent confrontations:

1. **Take a breath.** When a situation is happening now, it is hard in the moment, to step back and take a breath. But practice assessing the total situation before responding. Taking nice, slow, measured breaths calms the body in stressful situations.

2. **Listen**: Poor communication skills are often the mother of violent confrontations. When two people are talking loudly or violently at each other, who is listening? Exercise listening skills; make sure you understand what the person is saying.

3. **Ask for clarification**. If you don't understand what the person is saying ask. Replay his or her words back: "So let me see if I

understand what you are saying . . . or What I hear you saying is . . ." When you ask questions or restate the speaker's words back to him or her, it tells them that you are listening.

4. **Measure your words carefully.** "Speak softly but carry a big stick," words eloquently spoken by Theodore Roosevelt, the 26th President of the United States. When you address the issue, avoid speaking to quickly. Instead, speak softly but confidently in your words and your opinion.

5. **Avoid facial expressions and watch your body language**. You want the listener to concentrate on what you are saying not how you are saying it.

6. **Avoid anticipating your next response.** If you are thinking about what you are going to say, are you listening?

7. **Walk Away.** Don't turn your back on them while they are speaking. But rather agree to disagree and let it go. Ask yourself is this worth it? 9 times out of 10 it's not, so breathe easy and let it go.

8. **Stay Humble**. Anger is negative energy that can spread like wildfire. An inward smile can kill that negativity and give you the power to stay humble and implement steps 1-7.

Questions for Consideration:

1. Why am I angry?

2. What triggers my violent reactions?

3. How has my violent attitude or actions hurt me?

4. How have they hurt others?

LESSON 6

Repair and Reunite

Over the last few weeks, you have been considering yourself in relationship to the world. Re-examining the mistakes you made and working towards avoiding making the same costly mistakes once you leave have been the core concepts of this group. The next lesson asks you to take positive action towards others. The most important institution one can belong to is his or her family. Family provides a sense of belonging, gives unconditional love, and offers stability. Family whether it is the traditional family structure or an assembled family unit provides hope. But just like any institution there are rules. Your actions hurt people in your family; consequently, trust is destroyed, communication is weak, and love while present, it is fragile. It is not up to your family to repair the damage, it is up to you.

When a person leaves jail he or she should resolve to never return. Those who successfully keep that promise do so because they not only have a strong conviction against returning but also because they have fostered a healthy, stable support system. These individuals will not only seek forgiveness, but also contribute to a healthy family structure by establishing open lines of communication, avoiding unhealthy or negative relationships, and taking positive steps towards finding gainful employment and contributing successfully to his or her family and the community. A stable family environment is an important force in the rehabilitation of the ex-offender.

Understanding your role:

Family reunification is when individual(s) repair the damage done in the relationship by communicating honestly with one another in order to restore the family unit.

Communication cannot be one-sided each must listen through the tears and the pain. Therefore shouting is kept to a minimum and listening is essential. Do you hear your family member? Does he or she hear you? Your role is to facilitate this process.

Exercise sound judgment by staying focused on your goal: to reunite with my family, to forgive and be forgiven for past transgressions, and to re-establish trust and build healthy, nurturing relationships with my loved ones.

Be Patient:

You have done a lot of damage to your family. The disappointment, mistrust, and hurt have accumulated over the years. There is a lot of damage to undo. Therefore be prepared to accept the fact that all or some of your family may not be as quick to forgive you as you'd like for them to be. The damage is deep. You cannot uncover a band-aid without considering the depth of the wound. It is impossible to avoid. In this sense, so is internal pain your family is feeling towards you. Every day you are away, is compound interest added to their pain; they have learned to survive with it. Now you are asking them to accept that you've changed and are ready to be a better person. It's a heavy question that you are asking them. Think about it. Would be willing to accept a person's apology after years of mental, verbal, or even, physical abuse? Would be able to accept a person's apology who promised to be the financial provider only to be neglectful in his or her duties? Would you be so quick to accept a person's apology that has lied repeatedly to you? Chances are you would not. In other words, doubt and hesitation are normal. Be prepared to answer questions, be prepared to offer honest explanations, and be prepared for doubt to creep in until the individual (s) are sure that you have changed or are at least trying.

Be the Change you seek!

In jail or in prison, everyone has a made up mind to do better when he or she leaves, but the reality is very few do. A primary reason for this is that he or she lacks the trust and the faith in his or her self to make that change once they are on the outside. That is normal and understandable; it is easy to tell yourself you are going to change while incarcerated and another thing to do it once you are free. Old habits die hard.

In order to plant positive seeds of change, you must unearth the negative, deeply rooted seeds planted inside. Seeking the love and support of your family will also reaffirm trust and belief in self. You are your family and they are you. You all are individuals that exist within a whole. Repairing the cracked or fractured seals and healing the pain, will strengthen you as much as it will help them.

At this point in time, you are incarcerated. This is your truth today. Tomorrow, you will be free. Once you leave here, the challenge begins to stay true to the plan you've created while here. Along the way, there will be people that you will have to answer to about your actions. Most likely, your family, whose love and support you seek. Time to man or woman up: your family needs you and you need them. Repair and reunite with your family and move forward.

Questions for Discussion:

1. Family members whom I have disappointed, hurt, or victimized are (list your family members)

2. What is your role in the unhealthy relationships with your family?

3. How did you family hurt you?

4. I need my family because . . .

WEEK 7

Changing Behaviors (Life Skills)

The hardest thing for many ex-offenders to do is avoid repeating the same mistakes he or she made that led them to jail or prison in the first place. While behind bars, he or she will make promises to his or her self to avoid getting locked up again. It's easy to do while locked up; the reality of confinement is sobering to even the most reckless individuals. However, once on the outside the challenge and lure of a past life and old behaviors can be a strong temptation to resist. But resist you must. If you are going to be who you wish to become, you will need to fight off old behaviors and move forward.

Three areas that must change are language, mindset, and objectivity. In other words, the things you say, the things you think, and remaining open.

Language: Everything on you talks. It might not open its mouth but it talks: facial expressions, body movements, gestures, physical appearance, and even a person's health speak volumes about/for him or her. Think about it: What is a person who wears saggy jeans into an interview saying? Or a person who crosses his/her arms in a meeting, what is he/she saying? Not much? You are right—saggy jeans may symbolize something in jail or prison, but outside prison, it suggests that this individual is "hood" or does not care about his/her appearance. A person sitting with folded arms suggests to the observer that he or she is not listening or receiving the message of the speaker, just as out on the athletic court, a person who is slumped over is usually out of breath and probably tired. Your body, your movements, and your mind speak for you.

The Power of Language: Furthermore, what's felt on the inside is projected on the outside. If you tell yourself you can't do it, you won't; if you tell yourself you aren't worth much, and then you won't be. If you tell yourself, you are a part of a gang and cannot leave, and then you won't. If you tell yourself you are a good criminal . . . well, take a look around you, are you? It's clear that you are not being honest with yourself. The first step therefore is to take a look at how you see yourself: What does your body language say about you? What does your conversation (to others or to yourself) say about you? How can you change your language on the inside and out?

Mindset: This entire series has been about changing the criminal mind. Sometimes that is hard to do when the only person you are listening to is you. You exist in a bubble of one. When you live in a bubble of one—you are subject to tell yourself things to make you feel better about your circumstance. While you are incarcerated, you are in a bubble, sure you want to get out and do better, but if you do not take steps to work on getting better while inside, how can you do it, when you are on the outside? Change your mind. Your mind is your ultimate tool—you carry intellect, provide motivation, and use your five senses from this area. Read or create positive affirmations to strengthen your image of yourself. Find a spiritual avenue of expression: song, prayer, or meditation—feed your mind good energy and positive thoughts will flow. Remove negativity from your environment: get rid of negative people, avoid your old "stomping grounds," and try new things. In order to change your mind, you have to feed it with new things. Don't be afraid to try. Don't be afraid to step outside of your comfort zone.

Objective: Plain and Simple. Objectivity means that you remain open. It means understanding that there is more than your point of view. It means understanding that if you fail, you have to try again. Objectivity requires you remain open to change. It means that if someone has a differing point of view than yours, it's okay. You are entitled to your opinion and he or she is entitled to theirs. Objectivity is challenging because it is asking you to step outside of yourself and see others and yourself in a different way. Stay positive. Everyone is not going to see the new you immediately, but if you keep working at it he or she will.

Questions for Discussion:

1. Why is it important for the criminal to work on changing his or her mind while in prison?

2. What steps could he or she take while incarcerated to step outside of his or her comfort zone?

3. How can you keep an open mind about new ideas?

4. What kinds of positive things do you tell yourself to stay motivated about starting a new life? Why is this important?

5. "Not all those who wander are lost." What does this phrase mean to you?

LESSON 8

Enough is enough

At some point an individual must choose to move on. The past is exactly where it needs to be: behind you. Choose not to look back. Choose not to let it continue to torment you. You have the power to choose now. However, until you make the decision to move forward you will be stuck in the past.

Don't be afraid of moving forward. Change is good. In change there is growth. Fear contains. Fear holds an individual hostage by keeping him or her afraid of taking positive action in changing his or her life. Recognize fear and face it. Tell yourself: *I am better than my circumstance. I am able to change in the face of my fears; I am able to rise above the challenges yet to come because I believe in myself."*

Now is the time to say ENOUGH! I am changing. I am letting go of my past life and my negative thinking. I am moving forward because I have had enough.

Questions for Discussion:

1. What is your enough?

2. How are you going to change your life?

3. When I leave here I plan on making the following changes to my life:

LESSON 9

Successful People vs. Unsuccessful People

Your attitude is the difference between Success and Failure.

You are currently locked up. This is a failure on your part as your freedom as been stripped from you. It's a failure, because the last day you woke as a free man, you did not expect that the next morning as an incarcerated one. The county has you, and next time it may be the state or the federal prison. Which no one knows, that is uncertain, but what is certain is if you continue doing the same things you've always done, you will get what you've always got.

Below are a few ways to fail and few suggestions to achieve success.

How to fail at life:

❖ Negative Thinking: The way you see the world and your relationship to it determines how far you go in life. Your thinking can be your own worst enemy. Your thoughts determine whether you can or you can't. Try changing your thinking from negative to positive. You can do it merely by thinking but actions reinforce the positive thoughts.

❖ Failure to Plan: If you don't plan, have you created a plan? Yes. A failure to plan is a plan to fail. All success stories began with a plan. Just relying on your mind, will not ensure success. Sit down and create a realistic plan. Create a plan A and a plan B.

❖ Failure to Execute: It is not enough to plan. One must act. Unsuccessful people will sit around waiting for life to happen to them instead of them happening to it. Once you create a plan, execute it. Practice being consistent in your plans. Work on it every day. Chart your goals and your progress. This will reinforce positive thinking. When you see your results you feel good.

❖ Failure to Believe (The Faith Factor): The biggest mistake many unsuccessful people make is they fail to believe in themselves. As a result, they cannot accomplish goals because they fail to believe that they can. Every successful person will tell you the first person they believed in was themselves.

Questions for Discussion:

1. How do I see myself?

2. What are my plans once I am released?

3. How will I execute them?

4. How can I change my thinking from negative to positive?

5. Why is it better to be proactive instead of reactive? How does this help successful people?

LESSON 10

Pre-Release Preparation Part I

Recidivism refers to tendency to repeat. It is the repetition of poor behaviors or negative behaviors that ultimately lead to a return to jail or to prison. Your primary goal once leaving jail should be to never return, to avoid recidivism. It's safe to say that many people who are incarcerated and released have that goal. Unfortunately, many fail to reach their objective. Statistics suggest that 4 out of 10 prisoners upon release will return to jail within his or her first 3 years.* The primary reason an ex-offender will repeat old behavior is because he or she lacks the proper mindset or skills necessary for success.

Act now to avoid falling into the trap. Old behaviors are easy to slip into without a plan for success.

Tips to avoid recidivism:

1. **Develop a realistic plan.** Your reality is that you've made some mistakes that have landed you in jail or prison. Upon release, you are an ex-offender. The plan is to avoid becoming a repeat offender. Start today by first identifying the challenges to your success.

2. **Set short measurable, obtainable goals** that will lead to a long term objective. For example: 4 weeks upon my release, I will have my resume and cover letter developed, researched and applied to companies that hire ex- offenders. A chart is a good way to visualize the goals. See Below.

4-Week Plan	Goal:
Week 1: Reconnect (Get Functioning)	Phone, Professional Email, ID, GA, SSDI
Week 2: Reconnect/Research Important to identify and map out, which to apply to	Continue with week 1 goals and research ex- offender friendly companies and whose hiring
Week 3: Connect with Employment Specialists	Draft Cover Letter and Functional Resume
Week 4: Job Search	Put in a minimum of 5 applications (a week until employed)

3. **Eliminate the Negative:** Avoiding negative habits and behaviors means that you will have to eliminate some family members and friends. Replace them by making connections with positive people (family and new friends). Remember everyone cannot see your vision. You might receive negative backlash from your family and friends who you avoid. It's not personal or even about them. It's about you making a positive change in your life.

Other areas to consider:

1. Education: If you need a GED or are interested in returning to college, contact your local EDD. Or talk to a college counselor, most will help you navigate your way through the college process or even obtaining a GED.

2. Clothing: If you are short on money and lack clothing for a professional image. Contact your local Good Will or St. Vincent DePaul's. Often non-profit agencies such as this will

either have clothing or connect you with a non-profit who does.

3. Learn your Community: Many times there are local non-profits that provide job development, professional enhancement, or resume services for free. Contact your local Library. The librarian should be able to provide you with the information you need.

4. NA and AA: If you are in recovery or seeking assistance with recovery. Contact the local NA and AA groups before pursuing a job. Many times, these services may be able to assist you in your process. Often, these groups provide good networking opportunities.

Final Word

Stay positive. You are about to embark on the hardest journey of your life. You've made the decision to change your life for the better in a positive way. It's not going to be easy, but it is possible. Just stay the course and believe in yourself. Anything worth having is worth the pain it takes to achieve it.

Questions for Discussion:

1. What are you long term goals?

2. What are your short term goals? What would a Chart look like?

3. What are your current barriers to success?

4. I can overcome them by _____.

LESSON 11

Stage One: Job Readiness

Job Readiness

There are three stages when conducting a successful job search. The first is job readiness; the second is job search; and the final, is employment. This is a sequential process; each step prepares you for the next step. Preparing to enter the work force is the first stage. Job readiness is the first step in determining whether or not you are ready to become gainfully employed.

Understanding who you are and What you Want are Important.

Determine your likes and dislikes. What are you interested in? Where do you think you'd like to work based on those interests? If you enjoy animals, try the zoo. If you don't like working with the general public, avoid applying for McDonald's. Choose your field of interest.

Identify Your Goals:

It is important to set an objective. Why do you want to work? Where do you hope your employment will take you? Make your goals doable. Don't set a goal of being a millionaire in six months. That is an unrealistic goal. Instead set short goals that you can accomplish. Look at your career choice as a way to accomplish your short term goals.

Change your Mindset:

One of the key areas of conducting a successful job search is changing your mindset. You cannot go into an interview thinking the same way you do today. Street smarts, behavior, and dress, do not always transfer over well in corporate America. Therefore watch your language (profanity is not professional), curtail your swag (walk confidently without the excess body language) and pull up your pants (Appearance is always first. Invest in a belt. Ladies avoid colored hair and outrageous hairstyles.) Know that navy blue and black are appropriate colors for an interview.

Identify your Strengths:

Now that you've identified your field of interest and your goals, determine your strengths. How are prepared are you to work in your career choice? Is more training required? What do I bring to the table? How can I be an asset to the company? If more training is required, don't be afraid of school. You can also ask if the job offers training. Be honest with yourself as this will help you identify just how ready you are.

Research your Field:

What are the job qualifications? How well do you fit the requirements? What kinds of preparation have you had? Understand not just the field, but also the company's mission and goals. How well do you fit their objectives?

Prepare a Resume:

Nowadays competition is fierce in the work force. Consult a job developer or a resume builder and create a resume. Remember that the first insight the employer has into who you are is your resume and cover letter. For people with gaps in his or her history, the *functional resume* focuses on the applicant's skills and experience, rather than on his or her chronological work history.

Practice your Interviewing Skills:

Even the most qualified person for a job has to practice interviewing from time to time. Websites on the Internet provide questions that a potential interview might ask you, download them, and then practice your responses. Make sure to make good eye contact and always be truthful.

Above all stay positive.

Searching for a job can be a daunting challenge especially if you have been out of the work force for a long time. The key is to stay prepared and stay positive. Keep your long term and short term goals in mind. Everyone has to start at the bottom: today's dish washer is tomorrow's chef.

Questions for Discussion:

1. What are your interests? In which type of field do you think you'd enjoy working?

2. What are your short term goals? What are your long term goals?

3. Why is changing your mindset important to success outside of jail?

4. What are your strengths? What are your weaknesses?

LESSON 12

Learn to Live Stress Free

Everyone handles stress differently: What are your stressors? What causes you to worry and become anxious? What can you control? It is important that you handle stress in a fashion that is constructive for a happy and healthy life.

The following are tips to help you relieve stress:

1. **Meditate:** Sit up straight with both feet on the floor. Close your eyes. Concentrate on self. Practice releasing negative energy from the body, by releasing your mind from thought. Replace it with a positive mantra: *I love me. I am in a good place.*

2. **Breathe Deeply:** Take a few measured breaths that allow you to feel the inhalation and exhalation. A five-minute break to focus on your breathing negates the effects of stress and is known to lower blood pressure. Inhale through your nose and exhale through your mouth.

3. **Focus your Energy:** Be present in the moment by taking time to focus on the sensation of one sense: enjoy silence, enjoy the

warmth of the sun, enjoy walking, or enjoy a single delicious bite of food.

4. **Get Connected:** Spending time with others in your circle who are positive can send out positive vibes. Confide in someone you can trust. It's a great stress reliever.

5. **Get Aware:** Tune into your body. Wiggle your toes, flex your fingers, rotate your shoulders. Stress affects the each area differently, walking in awareness of this will help you to nurture each area and thereby relieve the stress.

6. **Unwind:** At the end your day, take a long shower or bath. Relax your shoulders as the beads of hot water touch your skin. Massage your calves, your thighs, your arms, and massage your neck. Close your eyes and rub your temples let your mind and your body relax.

7. **Write it Out:** Keeping a journal is a pure way to relieve stress. Chronicling your thoughts gives you a platform to get it out in private.

8. **Music Wonderland:** Listening to music is a great stress reliever. Put on your favorite artist and let you mind go. Dance a while or just lay there and relax. Allow your body the opportunity to escape in the melody.

9. **Work it Out:** Movement is a great stress reliever. Exercise: dancing, walking, or jogging are all good ways to relieve stress. Yoga is recommended, too. Learning to stretch the body while freeing the mind can be a good opportunity to relieve you from stress.

10. **Laugh:** Laughter is good for the soul. It helps to relieve tension that causes stress. The saying goes, Learn to laugh at life, cause if you don't life will laugh at you.

Finally, **Have an Attitude of Gratitude:** Be grateful for all of the good things. Let the negative things go. Remember negative energy holds you back. Positive energy drives you forward.

Questions for Discussion:

1. What external factors affect your environment?

2. How can you eliminate them?

3. What steps can you take in your life to become stress free?

4. How can you change your attitude about your situation?

5. What are you grateful for?

LESSON 13

Pre-Release Preparation Part II:
Creating the Master Plan

In lessons 1-4, you examined your life: how you got here and what steps you are going to take once you get released. In Week 10, you looked at ways to de-stress. This week we are going to strategize. By developing practical, purposeful steps you can redirect your destiny. The end goal should not be county jail, state or federal prison; it should be a life full of expectancy. You are in control of your destiny and now is the time to create the master plan to make it happen.

In lessons 4 and 10, you were provided with an overview for change upon release. Completing those charts gave you an idea of how to create change in your life. This week we are going to create a master plan. A master plan should be thought of as the plan for future success once you leave jail. It should be a detailed list of your objectives and goals; with a realistic timeline for completing them.

Developing a doable plan is a major key to success.

The following are 7 steps for creating a sound plan:

1. **Establish a Goal.** A plan is based on a goal, an objective you are striving to achieve. There are two types of goals you should set. The longer goal, which is the overall objective; this is the longer term goal. The shorter goals are shorter measurable goals that take a lesser amount of time to achieve.

2. **Action plan.** After identifying short measurable goals, breakdown each short goal into action plans. Consider what steps it will take for you to complete each goal. What actions do you need to take?

3. **Build a Timeline:** After you have completed the action plan, the next step is to build a timeline. How long will it take for you to accomplish each goal? A good way to approach this step is to consider how much time you have. While time is important, avoid making costly mistakes by rushing your goals. Create a realistic time line by being honest with yourself.

4. **Understand your Money:** What financial assets are available to you? Where is your money flow coming from? What is your concrete money (money that you have access to) and what is your soft money (money that is a possibility)?

5. **Be Proactive:** Troubleshoot any possible problems that you might incur ahead of time. Usually these are barriers to your success like lack of ID (valid), access to Social Security Card or a birth certificate, a car, and/viable transportation.

6. **Measure your success:** Sometimes it's hard to see your success. It is good practice to mark your success. In step 3, you build a timeline. Use it as a tool to measure your success.

7. **Time for Action:** After completing steps 1-6, it's time for action. You are now ready to put your plan into action.

Example:

Long Term Goal: To Reconnect with My Family

Short Term Goal	Measurable	Timeline	Goal Complete
Week 1: Get Used to my Settings	Understand the facility: rules, protocol	Week 1/ ongoing	Yes—I am ready for Week 2
Week 2: Establish a money source: Apply for GA.	Make contact with Social Services-	Week 1 or 2	Yes/No Contacted GA/ Need to get ID

Note: Each week you set and accomplish a goal, check it as complete. Make sure to add any additional notes that you may need to fully accomplish it. The writer in Week 2 contacted GA but needs his or her ID before completing it. Next week's goal is to get the ID and return to GA. Remember it may take some time to complete each goal but by charting your progress, you are able to see what you've accomplished.

Your Chart:

Long Term Goal:

Short Term Goal	Measurable	Timeline	Goal Complete
Week 1:			
Week 2:			
Week 3:			
Week 4:			
Week 5:			
Week 6:			

LESSON 14

What's Your Purpose?

Over the last 12 weeks, you've examined your life. In the first 6 weeks, you've considered the choices you've made and how they have impacted you and others. You've also asked forgiveness from yourself and seek forgiveness from others you've hurt while in your pain. In the latter half of the program, you continued to work on yourself by considering your future. Once you are free from incarceration, you don't have to make the same choices that landed you here. You are free to change your mind and move forward in a different direction. The external forces: family, friends, environment, education (lack of), employment, etc., do not have to drag you down. You have the power to change. You have the power to walk away so you can improve yourself and your station. Jail does not have to be a lifetime choice, you have the power to end the cycle and move forward.

Life happens. It happens to everyone who lives. People may not experience it the way you do, but it happens to them just the same. The difference between them and you is attitude. Are you going to fight and do something better or are you going to give into negative thinking? The "I-can't-attitude" or the fear factor, are attitudes and excuses that are holding you back. You and how you see life and your role in it is the common denominator. You have the power to do something positive with yourself for the benefit of yourself and others. You have the power within you to be a light in your community.

Everyone has a purpose in life. It is a part of your higher calling. Think about it. There is something that you've always wanted to do. Why are you here? It's not being a criminal, because that choice landed you in jail. Today jail. Tomorrow prison. Face it. You are not a good criminal. Isn't time to think about something different?

Fear is natural. Be afraid and change anyway. You are responsible for your future. You are a better person than your current circumstance, when you exit these four walls that currently have you confined, plan on doing something better for yourself and for the world around you.

Questions for Discussion:

1. What is the purpose for my life?

2. How can I make a difference in my life and the lives of others?

3. How can I avoid returning to jail?

4. I am empowered by _____.

FINAL THOUGHTS

Congratulations on completing the 14-lesson plan to becoming a better you. Success is in your hands. Stay positive and motivated in reaching your goals. Feed your spirit positive energy and watch the world move aside for you. It's possible, several before you have successfully changed their lives.

Positive recitations like this mantra will help you achieve your goals. Just believe.

Today is the first day of the rest of my life. I am going to change for the better, so I can live a healthy, more productive life. I am motivated to make a difference in my life, my family, and my community. I am determined to turn my beliefs into my reality.

Good luck on your journey!

Change Your Criminal Behavior: One Day at a Time.

BIBLIOGRAPHY

A Guide to Creating Your Life Plan. In Life Optimizer. Retrieved on August 14, 2014. *http://www.lifeoptimizer.org/2009/04/07/create-your-life-plan/*

Image retrieved on November 14, 2014 from: *http://www.livethegreatescape.com/wp-content/uploads/2012/11/ball_n_chain_freedom_800_clr.png*

Job Search Tips in Career One Stop. Viewed on July 14, 2014. *http://www.careeronestop.org/reemployment/jobsearchhelp/job-search-tips.aspx*

http://www.pewtrusts.org/uploadedFiles/wwwpewtrustsorg/Reports/sentencing_and_corrections/State_Recidivism_Revolving_Door_America_Prisons%20.pdf

Rivera, Luis. De-escalation: The Art of Avoiding Violence.

http://www.endesastres.org/files/The_best_way_to_deal_with_violence_is_to_avoid_it_1_.pdf

Roosevelt, Theodore. *http://www.brainyquote.com/quotes/quotes/t/theodorero130674.html*

http://static.nicic.gov/Library/025057/default.html

http://en.wikipedia.org/wiki/Psychosocial

Copies of this booklet are available in Spanish and other languages upon request.

Written by Douglas McKoy, Jr.

Founder of *Changing Criminal Behaviors Consulting Services*

Contact me at:

P.O.Box 2377

Suisun City, CA 94585

Email: *CCBCSDMC@GMAIL.COM*

Phone: (510)708-4350

Changing Criminal Behaviors Consulting Services, LLC

Changing Criminal Behaviors:
One Mind at a Time.

November 12, 2014

Lightning Source UK Ltd.
Milton Keynes UK
UKHW012021080621
385174UK00008B/350/J